DELERE

FIRST PUBLISHED IN 2017 BY
DELERE PRESS LLP
370G ALEXANDRA ROAD
#09-09 SINGAPORE 159960
WWW.DELEREPRESS.COM
REG NO. T11LL1061K

ISBN   978-981-11-4568-1

PURE AND FAULTLESS ELATION EMERGING FROM HIDING

BY LIM LEE CHING
WITH DRAWINGS BY BRITTA NORESTEN

WITH AN INTRODUCTION BY NEIL MURPHY
AND AN AFTERWORD BY JEREMY FERNANDO

THE POEMS HAVE BEEN SEQUENCED
BY MARY ANN LIM & THE LAYOUT HAS BEEN
COMPOSED BY YANYUN CHEN

LIM LEE CHING : BOUNDED BY BEAUTY

BY NEIL MURPHY

Lim Lee Ching's poetry declines the easy target, refuses newspaperese logic, social diagnosis and other such *busy* topics. Instead, it announces itself with a white-light focus that only considers what is essential, poetic, and human. The necessary remove of the poet – what Denis Donoghue calls the poetic imperative of "autonomy, disinterestedness, and impersonality" – is everywhere evident here. Poem after poem display voices at once austere and full of focused intent, emotion carefully held in check, tension-filled. Yeats insisted that "all imaginative art remains at a distance and this distance, once chosen, must be firmly held against a pushing world," and Lim clearly belongs in such company. Echoes of the modernist masters are everywhere, particularly Yeats, Stevens and Pound, but they are here transplanted into a very distinct landscape.

If anything, Lim's poetry is even more pared down, more devoid of specific anchors to the social world, and filled with numerous swirling sequences, Joycean linkages, sentence loops, as in "Ode to Everman," which opens with a vortex of language drawing one to its centre:

> Twice two times once a second
> two times
>
> A return twin fates
> intertwined destinies

Surviving on one-two one-twos
hut
hurt

A tale
two
to beat the best of them

Twice raucous then silent then silent
beating always syncing
together as one

The words are at play with each other, dancing with each other in pursuit of the formal impact rather than merely scuttling after meaning – the poem "The Ballad of Ryan White" even reminds us of this in its refusal of "the fatal futility of fact" while another, "Bookmarks," even revels in "the stability of uncertainty" that a refusal of fixed meaning achieves.

Poems like "Full of care" ("And so God's sigh echoed, / Echoed as the spirits / Stand by the gates") extend the looped sense of words while throughout each speaker's voice offers a recalibration of the focus – from the surrender of authority to the reader's voice in the fill-in-the blanks mode of "quick guide" to the continual suspension of the emotional utterance, to the adoption of an invented persona, in "Unbound" in which "Men Jiang" speaks, "muddying history". Similarly, at times, the voice enters into a kind of overt intertextual ventriloquism, as in "Cull" which is more a variation on Yeats' "The Second Coming" than a simple example of influence. Yeats' intonations are instantly put to Lim's own uses:

> Waiting and baiting on the narrowing perch,
> The centre holds them still.
> A trunk, a branch – of streets and lanes,
> Of skinny legs and weathered shoulders.

Rather than a philosophical engagement with the cyclical rise and fall of civilizations, "Cull" inversely focuses on the specificity of meanness of spirit and petty arguments: "Desire will not teach the ignorant. / Who will teach their young / Of fight and flight". Lim's manner of engaging with his influences is a source of fascination in itself with allusions to Keats and Yeats nestled up against the presences of everyone from Warren Beatty to David Bowie – but always in a re-constituted way that speaks of a confidence that has long since moved beyond anxiety or mere admiration.

A particular favourite is "Bookmarks" – an extended meditation on beauty that may itself be read as a self-conscious detailing of Lim's own aesthetic:

> The lone walker hears the secrets of the wind and the
> voices of the trees.
> The path is not tongue-tied.
> Here, strong lines persist, incanting, singing.

The self-reflexive mirror that the poem holds up to
itself offers relentless commentary on poetic process
and the pursuit of beauty, all the while itself forging
lines that glow with their own value as poetry:

> Truth and beauty remain
> Of brush strokes and clean lines
> Leading the way and the coloured imaginings.
> Concealment and transgressions are such delicate gestures
> As are learning and gesturing.
> Only the words remain to be spoken, the writing to be sung
> Of happinesses witnessed and tongues tied
> In full contemplation of the idea of ideas.

At times the insistent, incantationary tone almost
devours itself;

> Keep the song burning, seared into meaningfulness
> Keep forgiveness as the dance to a measure of memory
> Keep aside an obsession over the might of imagination
> Keep courage in the light of what may be seen

Only to always return to the essence of it all – the
song, the dance, the edging forward:

> The voices chanting ancient thoughts and futuresongs of
> Fearful breaths of tender thoughts of
> The place of, the parts of dreams of
> Footsteps of dancesteps of songsteps of wordsteps.
> They edge closer on.

What a relief to encounter work so bereft of mere cant and noise, so alert to its own motivations, its own breath and movement, its own poetry. Lim Lee Ching's poems give cause to celebrate.

PURE AND FAULTLESS ELATION EMERGING FROM HIDING

BY LIM LEE CHING

ODE TO EVERMAN

Twice two times once a second
two times

A return twin fates
intertwined destinies

Surviving on one-two one-twos
hut
hurt

A tale
two
to beat the best of them

Twice raucous then silent then silent
beating always syncing
together as one
as you are

Boom time rolling rowing
a peace tensed at best
apiece each hand

Arms
holding
holding off hanging on

Impossible whispers
now merely silence

Armed
holding
beating beating away

Hounded
haunted
shadows long and lingering

Grinding
tales of possibility
possibilities

Safe now
saved possibly

By the twice
two times
almost always arriving

Arrived

MAYBE, BABY
(FOR WARREN BEATTY)

The ballroom yields upon entry of
the dashing, dashering figure glancing, certain
Ever the cravat advocate
Affirming glass portrait as scene stealer
One at a time
one at a time

Deep in, ever unsure, hope drenched in doubt
Deep in, the mask pains expectation into posture
One at a time one at a time

Starboard stutterings stay still
Words dissolving into knotted whispers
Of pretend goodbyes and good lord
Trading on the meeds of others
Unloading pomposity one at a time
One at a time

So certain
As to rhyme with a smile
Taking the orders of love
Upon the laps of conviction
Blinded, always blinded by the ordinates
Of certainty here, now
A picture of moving affectations
Inventing. Always inventing part after part and
one at a time

THE TAKING OF HOW MANY

The viscosity of sixes and sevens in Room
Eight, lines, twins and thirsties. There
Is no way of translating the ways of always
Exclaiming many to all. The
Sipping and singing keeps one and all from sinking
Into unnecessary feeling and thinking.
Yet it necessitates
Laughing in tears, crying at the smile of the one
Thought. Remembering the bright to dim lighting
Of six to two making eight. Hours
Can only be long-lasting night after numbing nights
Of unceasing celebrating, of ringing in for the
One lasting one more. Leaving, finally,
With the half-lights lingering.
Halved too far.

CULL

Waiting and baiting on the narrowing perch,
The centre holds them still.
A trunk, a branch – of streets and lanes,
Of skinny legs and weathered shoulders.

Desire will not feed the hungry.
The calm day light belies the ruffled nights,
The night masked the day
Of fight, of fright,
And frenzied feeding against stained walls.

No one knew when the armed men arrived.
All heard the sprays of delight,
Some muffled glee and much flight.
Lead and ladder reached the heights.
The sprays of resolution,
The sprays of anger and hatred and petty delight.

The descent followed shortly after.
Everyone a little death.

Desire will not teach the ignorant.
Who will teach their young
Of fight and flight?
In the evening, more returned
To wait and bait on their trembling perch.

THE BALLAD OF RYAN WHITE

In the end, we can only improve on the fatal futility
of fact.
If we know how.

The destructive love, they coiled
And recoiled, like sweetened tales
Of adder-ridden charms

In birth, in life,
In the breach of the lashing lights.
Those lights unleashing unrelenting promptings.
The fear – theirs – capsuled in
The moment of moments.

Contagion is a branded, brand new, sorrow.
It beats and heaves and heaves again,
In surviving, survived none – refused all.
It heaves and beats again.

The dusting of skin demanded ghastly grey,
As if flushed skin needs be infused with
Prognoses and judgement.

Here the intimations of intuition
Completes the cycles of confusion
And then heaves again, pricking conscience.
Only the facts remain.

AND IOWA IS ONE SYLLABLE

What, then, is the nature of this
Divine love with its vicious turn?

Sifting light from the
Impossibility of authenticity

Your pitch straining still as
A concession to the other

Utterances of the unsolvable
Pieces of darkness' blight

So, then, this is your
Penchant for pomposity

The scattering of intimate
Terseness

The weaves of an edge providing
These delights of heaping

Turn after broken turn
Always just always on the verge

At centre of your own quarrels
The unhurried descent lands

A pitch streaming beyond the lessons
And Iowa is one syllable

BOOKMARKS

The lone walker hears the secrets of the wind and the voices of the trees.
The path is not tongue-tied.
Here, strong lines persist, incanting, singing.
How does the judgement, what criteria persist
To keep the premise sound? It is written and shall be read.
The strong lines and certain doubts exact change.
It stands thus to reason that it shall be pleasing.
Truth and beauty remain
Of brush strokes and clean lines
Leading the way and the coloured imaginings.
Concealment and transgressions are such delicate gestures
As are learning and gesturing.
Only the words remain to be spoken, the writing to be sung
Of happinesses witnessed and tongues tied
In full contemplation of the idea of ideas.
Remember the rules of memory in order
That it may coolly be accorded its place in the deep space
Between the seeing and reading that these words demand.
They love a little strangeness in order to test the edges of conjecture.
For what loads more than the values of being just. In time
All that go long also go up as memory of fire.
Distance takes the soul off blame, off exclusion –
This is not the province of king, colonel or clown,
Nor the realm of whisperers seeking to please.
By rendering asunder, it is fused, conflated, returned to line.
Persistence is not learning. Persistence cannot be unlearned.
The foundations established by the building blocks of comprehension

May not be mere adagia – it must gather.
Distance dances preclude ordered methods, pleasing encryptions.
Choice is evaluated according to the cloths laid feet-down,
Not the testimony of pride.
Through this all there has been no escape from expanding doubt
Nor lessons in terminality.
In truth, the source of ignorance may well be reluctant pursuit.
The way to compulsion can come to close
As other delights arise, other lures
Drawing sight into the realm of perfect beauty.
The cult of stability and singular meaning
Diminishes ascendant beauty, delight and breath-hope.
Licence and liberty are only cloaks, nothing more.
Goose-steps are not hoof-taps – they do not tire,
And yet they dig on, scoring the spell onto meaning, onto a basis
For believing abjectly the sound of thoughtdepth.
Persistent therefores are fallacious,
They bind while unleashing the gateward push.
Suffer the testimony of pride
And branded pleasure that go right through the marrow of memory.
The mind and soul and limbs and heart be as one, as many,
Upward in glory of wishfulness on wings of wisdom.
This afterall is the race of consolation.
Victimhood has no sum but the total of contrivance,
As the two of the dance in waltzes in nines.
Trembling limbs hold aloft the taut words:
Lines stretching far into the north of a past.

There the hundred riders dance a little lick
Gathering up the pinned down sighs in marred frigidity,
Where lies a totality stretched in quarters and sixths.
And still the pleasing pulse beats to the long day.
Daring little steps of glancing thoughtspace.
Keep pace, keep apace of what is left and what refused.
The gleaming blade trembles and pierces
This fall of falls, with fireweed summerbreeze.
There is no death here, so no crying shoulders,
Only clumps of anxious logic to tap the rhythm of smoke.
To each his card, for each his hour
Which inching futureward relearns the songs of the leaves.
Wandering lost among the layers of liabilities,
Yet killing kindness with tiredness,
And beating and heating the song into submission.
Stealing into the angel's share takes shivering prayer
And flagellation as art.
The value of these words are weighted with the wages of sorrow,
These sculpted fingers must scratch through the layers of song.
Courage sings the scripted fear of expectation
To a reasoning halt, that where it seems, it may lay down.
Keep the song burning, seared into meaningfulness
Keep forgiveness as the dance to a measure of memory
Keep aside an obsession over the might of imagination
Keep courage in the light of what may be seen
Keep faith in the stability of uncertainty
Frailty can turn the cause on its front

Providing the cues for vain utterances.
The portion lost is the weight of ashes.
What favours might there be if the rendering is strained?
Dead words are buried yet mined again, with fervour.
Greenloops flourish in the presence of misapprehension
And are buried again. That heaviness is the weight of
Staggering mediocrity. In time, compasses no longer matter:
Nijinski is a shaman of the garden.
This covenant of words is a nightwish of a race.
Tied tongue insists the words be spoken, the songs sung
In praise of perfection or performance but not both.
Promises, too, can be sound and mean more as consolation.
Platitude in numbers cannot afford pound for pound
The exhaustion of footsteps.
Running with the cadence, the steps making ancient rhymes
That the earth has heard
Whispery songs of woven trances,
Of ancient wisemen oozing
From the dreambirth of each grain of land.
This then is the milk of silence.
What wine and nectar can sway is the surface of grudge?
Here are strong lines leading the way to repetition.
Was it a waltz?
What is left is truly the fragrance of remembrance.
The galloping meaningfulness raises the stakes of wisdom.
Go forth. Accord each a place in abjection.

Receive the supplication of some sincerity
In order to make vulnerability part of experience.
There is no trap but the trickery of reason.
Many as one, step dance song, heart soul, as one.
Before reading and seeing, the thought.
The long day stills the fleeting delight
Of whispers and sighs.
Beneath the lid of passion awakens the phrase
That locates far into the northward of trembling hope.
Here again a little strangeness.
It edges closer on.
Some pushing upward of a past
And now, here, strain the lines of a tender breath.
Weighting yet in seconds and quarters.
Suffer the testimony of vainglory.
The ancient turn completes the repetition of repetitions,
For the direction of time still matters.
Licence and liberty wear a face each
Meeting intimations of few favours.
Offering a posture for legacy,
In full contemplation of this thought of thoughts.
Sorrow is another hundred riders
Chancing out of the darkness into the bright.
The words shiver through these wet pages
As through the coldness of the mind forge.
Penance is the province of princes, not poor men.
These words shall be risen a warm body.

Warmed by the light of lights.
Here lies the awakening
Of the dispensation of an age,
Dismissing the certainty as one in many.
Enthusiasm catches on also as one
In the simplicity of essence and discernment.
Wrapped in the verses are triggers of
Silence that surround the seeing and hearing of
The voices chanting ancient thoughts and futuresongs of
Fearful breaths of tender thoughts of
The place of, the parts of dreams of
Footsteps of dancesteps of songsteps of wordsteps.
They edge closer on.
Trembling limbs hold on still to the taught lines,
Fearful of giving heart to the beauty of succumbing
To the presence of each moment.
The sheets of sound
And walls of light
Beat in quavers, quarter tones and half wits.
The secrets of the wind and voices of the trees
Enchant and sing, enchant and sing.
The lines are just and indeed persist.
What remains is the memory of hope,
The basis of many beliefs, not one.
Absolutes cannot be traded
For a hundred riders, nor another.
The faces put on meet the faces within,

Voices sing directly to the seeing eye that
Vanishes into the echoing wall of the hopes
For the tribe of promise – glancing as witness,
Observation as commitment to memory,
Carved onto the core of consciousness.
Bounded by beauty. As beauty.
Here, surrounded by these covers
Are the pages of the maker
Read.
The ancient turns complete the repetition of repetitions.
In full contemplation of a thought of thoughts,
A fall of falls, warmed by the light of lights,
In full contemplation of the idea of ideas.
It is a force unrelenting.
It is a force contagion.

SONG

The echoes that are never heard
Do not ever go away
They gather to the back of the heart
Where angels stay to play

The shadows of great height
Dance nights and return by day
To gather at the back of the heart
Where angels stay to play

The river of little hope
Yet rises to certainty's bay
It gathers to the back of the heart
Where angels stay to play

The children there learn no hate
For all is glorious and gay
And can, gather at the back of the heart
Where angels stay to play

The wisdoms burrowed now hatch
In ancient scripture and lay
As one gather to the back of the heart
Where angels stay to play

The great craftsmen toying before hearth
Deep warmth giving life to clay
Feet gather at the back of the heart
Where angels stay to play

The angels undo all hurt
Ensuring the seekers and the stray
Find their way back to the heart
Where angels stay to play

On the maker's table, the hymn
Echoes sacred praise
The players of the heart
Sing to glory and stop to pray.

FULL OF CARE

And so God's sigh echoed,
Echoed as the spirits
Stand by the gates, astirred,
Ready to gather stones
And jewels for the feast of
Appearances. Inside
The gathered marveled and
Wondered seeing seen, delight
At the delicateness
Of the sounds unseen,
Unmarked
Yet remarkable.
Lips taking sips,
Hips adjusting to catch the best
Of light. Flakes and films
Gather favour as the
Visitors stand fix footed
Under the lone tree,
Unmatched by
Unseasonable furiosity.
Flash after flash by.
And the mountain's cry shattered,
Shattered in between
Two stools of ash.
The frame-makers will mourn
As mirrors echo and
Again the seeming delight.

Reason because serious
Must not be literal
Only so the basis
Of belief may
Soothe the flashes of
Resounding points.
Sensibility capable
Of bursting into light.
And the night, starry and
Filled with glory and might
Takes towering breaths,
Whistling unto the blurred
Lines of the day's
Curiosity. Weaned off
By the angel's
Tupentinian whiff. And
The stones in the flame
Sparkle with the brightness
Of the hearts
Of the faithful.

ROAD RISES

Road rises, journey hurting the earth
With its wheeled steps. Outside the road rises.
Lured deeply into wonderment.
This is the cure for race. The champagne-
Coloured saloon lacks imagination
But the dashboard contention between
Plastic Jesus and battery Elvis
Turns tongue of spreading sorrow towards
The least relative point.

The village
Of sadness where caressing typist
Hands pick up smoking coals to drive the
Turning disc. Skulls kicked in by relentless
Words, dressed in tenderising songs of
Intents and suppositions. The native
Son returns to the deathbed of an age.

MEAL ON THE HILL

Do you have change for a fifty?
No. Why don't you pay when you come here the
next time?
But I don't live around here.
It's ok, you will come back.

– overheard

A difficult place to arrive at
Far from a stop, even obscured
The house sitting atop

They speak of the flavours of a place
Of the here and sometimes
Of nothing rushed

Efforts have to be made
To inherit the parts that matter
Some even known to weep

Amid drizzles of tears and taste
Many an ordered credulity
Affirmed by the agreement

Of others who would declare
Allegiance to alternative
Choices and dictates

Textures and echoes
Rarely, barely described
Every gesture a completion

Nearby, the picking resumes
Doubles and triples
Packing and return.

SHALLOWBREATH

我不相信天是蓝的，
我不相信雷的回声，
我不相信梦是假的，
我不相信死无报应。

－ 北岛，"回答"

Cartwheels turning uptown, by doors of warm eyes
Staring ribboned arches on loops and flutters
Signs only point, warm turn taking off in buried shifts
The ages contest on settled sons who would
Only cast each turn as short as startles can carry
More. More controls of load and landing
Skipper takes stage left, pricking ears to a frayed linen
And more, much left to run the piping dry
Such winded depths are a cause for troubled rest
But so too the morning's secrecies
How far can the hands reach in? How tight the grasp?
Till it flows. Upwards as certainty parses
Threads on the sheets give way to the utterance
Of the cobbled many. Who lays this side of the
Angled holstery; who assembles the felt needs
Of the meddled few. These strains calls
Forth the west-bound harp snitches of
A celebrated warmth. A textiled nursing of
Allayed smokememory. Assigned parcels
And so passes the rolls of uptown cartwheels
Hours displaced upon hours on each turn upwards
Line, thread. Invitations to tea
Twinnings and silver plates. Tables for tanned
Elbows. How hard had they driven; how harm's
Length hounded the highroad venture, forcing sighs
That recent memory can only address. Damp
Surroundings are an easy answer to the strides

Outward-here. Can sally comeward attend to
The stilled sheets under which length-bound
Tangled-tot come hussle forth? Skipper takes the left
This night the doors of warm eyes remain
Drenched with the naked anguish of generations
Of the driven. Whose shopping bags hold
Up the sky's share of the starry eyed ribbon gasps
Far enough to reach the end of another side
Of a deep, gruelling stained call to hussle forth
Who's left is left in need, in ankle deep
Step wheels, raking defied yard work, heading
Height-ward. Go within blinking distance from
The shared symptoms of ribbon loop
This band is your sand, this hand is your stand
So the next day's planned concessions
Let go of pan dust gathered against withdrawn
Efforts. Plain sight portending the degrees
Of enveloping figurations one to every
Tanned elbow and broad shoulder burdened
With the load of answer and belief
As horsemen pass by scattering the season's
Blind dust for the early call to muster
Musts up the modest clearing with murmurs
To stir the humanity off the earth of deposited
Pleasantries. Ablemen and their worthies
Take heart to every accumulated sense
And interest in the blessed return to

Wish making. The night saw off the rest that
The fitful can find scarce in the deep-scented
Deep-land that must now count as settled
Redress. Crossroads are so founded
In the venerable age, by the venerable
Bodyside, the worshipful take heart in the blessed
Return. To wish, to heal, to prayer, to the
Word of a winded thread upon to hang every
Utterance of civil obedience. Fervour is faint
Determinant but gives to the seeing
Eye the reverie of a poet's clear breath and
Silent counting of the beat steps towards the
Imagined hooftaps of distant invitations
Can the sink light for once provide the useable
Words of fateful apprehension? Who sought the
Kissing bay left of the half-tracked stamping
Line, invites the heart-plaids of the sole
Tethered stand man? Hurtled onwards to
The marrow of the morning might. Had the brush
Strokes arrived earlier, the scheme would yet
Weather down to the prayerful tears of
The hand clasped stone catchers who coat
The rich earth's manners with far more than
Weariness. Blue clouds, the days ahead will
Roll onwards, heaven by. The sixth prayer
Not to be found. The ardour of obedience claims
Admission to the persistent front end

Where all is wonder, want not more than
Lofty strides among the streaming tea tide
Prayer for prayer, accuracy's demands count many
To exclude those who have fallen deep into the
Spell of words, seeds and pollen grain aloft
Pitch, trunk and wide arms. Skyward, all seem
All seeing, all introspection, all oddly
Calmed despite the horror of hope destining
Divining from castaway pebbled path of knee high
Supplicating. Knowing depth of the valleys of
Survival at the edge of the earth's conceit and rhyme
Nothing holds still beyond the line. Nothing and
Everything biding pulse for pulse, shattering the
Din of the key of night. Of completed eagerness
To please the shrine and keeper, gate and key
All, all who seek this night and moons to come
Cast not shadow cast not stony fitless stare
Of those there, and all absent, sent inwards
Staring ribboned arches by the door of warmed eyes.

[UNTITLED]

and then there was light
and so there was beauty
and there was all
and so there was loyalty
and then there was rest
and so there was always
and then there was turn
and so there was right
and then there was remnant
and so there was chance
and then there was time
and so there was extent
and then there was reach
and so there was touch
and then there was pull
and so there was nearness
and then there was safety
and so there was shelter
and then there was rest
and so there was use
and then there was more
and so there was joking
and then there was laughing
and so there was feeling
and then there was loving
and so there was you
and then there is you

QUICK GUIDE

first blue dark ripe new fast
big wide dry dumb clean sound
weak white black nice fair long
worst warm flat lush smooth bright
loud tired small brash stiff tame
camp hot drab late tense bad
red short crisp best tough mad
class stale fine dire wise sad
cold soft plain hard top lame
fresh smart proud grave dull light
gold slow pale fun young strong
green sharp rough full good round
dim firm sweet free large last

Sometimes a show can be too_____for its own good. Where it displays a _____ talent for the _____, this piece, which is being performed in accompanying matinee and late-evening performances, feels as if it is pushing too much into a _____ space. _____ is not always _____ .

Yet even with so _____ a profile, the artist feels _____ _____ to divisions between the more _____ , _____ _____ traditions. Even the cynic will admit they are _____ , as _____ in _____ , _____ articulation as in _____ , _____ power. Some of repertoire might be _____ at moments, but these performers make it   _____ .

Despite its production issues, this is a _____ revival of the original. It shows a _____ talent at its most _____ _____ and has the feel of a _____ classic.

On the surface, the show looks like a _____ treatment of _____ integrity. In true _____ fashion, the artist complicates the issue in several ways. And it's a measure of subtlety that we are shown how even the most _____ art can be co-opted by the _____ intentions.

Much of the intent is _____ to the audience, and the atmosphere around the opening suggests that it was ready for something _____. While its concept has a _____ resonance, there's a _____ inevitability in the handling of it that makes for _____ returns. The difference between conceptual art and theatre may all be in the timing.

The audience had a _____ time as the show, brilliantly conveying a shift from _____ to _____ with _____ artists. The lead, in a _____ role in _____ gear, pins down the _____ power of the establishment.

With _____ sets that evoke the _____ nature of the setting without actually showing it, this is a production that does __ _____ engagement with the show and makes _____ of any suggestion that the artist had sold out.

The artist comes up with some _____ images. But the __ _____ of the format means it is _____ to explore the _____ ideas in depth. In short, the show is too _____ _____ to make any _____ impact. And, although it is _____ _____ staged, it left the audience feeling _____ rather than _____.

It quickly becomes clear that part of the idea is to use humour to send up some of the _____ attitudes still dominant in the art world. So, the pleasures of discipline are extolled, the players get their turn and pretentiousness gets a _____ kicking.

What sets this work apart from other others is the _____
 with which it uses the idiom to circumscribe the agitation. Technically
this is a very _____ cast but in the end it is _____
 timing that carry the performance. It has the _____
and the _____ of a _____ warmth
that carries the audience with it every step of the way.

PREPARATIONS

And how they bought their positions
With saccharin and trust
And the world was asleep
To our latent fuss
- David Bowie, "The Bewlay Brothers"

I
Shining bright, a whim of the waning day cast on waves
Bathed in the shallow breaths of an ancient yearning
Cast low, our shadows stretch through the fingertips of dreams
Dusk after distant dusk
Not having glanced beyond these clear lines
The searing only ever stand us on ceremony
With empty rituals emptying past the tips of keenness
Moving lips in restless halls echoing the tips of keenness
Taking a stand against the flood of querulous envy
Everywhere it exposes the yawning need
For the stamp of our acquiescence
Tip on tip, hip to hip, the meaningful blast
Of these unsung verses
Relocate the calculation of rests

II
A return begins before fading back to the shadows of fulfilment
In village after village, the mews defy the gathering circus
Who comes, who shines, greeting with raised hairlines
Kicking off the dust beneath old papers and dead news

Surely rest must come to bully the outstretched body
Limp to the touch of dim dusk
Turning on the ash of forgotten scribbled sheets
The words gather lightly on the lips
As if returning to the day of toil
Watching the shadow grasping towards the wall's end
The words on the lips listing adjacent melodies
Lips searching for a near-rhyme
To cast aside the waning day for the night

III
Day breaks, the memory of marsh past buried
Beneath these layers of enhanced hoof taps
Surely, the badge is a mark of primal logic
It pierces the truths we left behind when the stroll
Became the goose steps of a dreaded generation
The searing only ever stand us on ceremony
With rituals emptying into parades of worshipful ghosts
The soil wields to the tired heels
As if returning to its days of buried memories

IV
Enter the great swathes of turning attitudes
Where the root notes of our instincts
Take a stand against envy
Unlayering the stubborn peels of forward face
The carrier asks no questions, only holds up an end

Of the bargain
Keenness is a light that cannot be blinked away
Just as the shifting sand of petty shillings
Give way to stagger and appetite
Day breaks and the grip on buried memory
Is sustained by the sighs of a generation wedded
To the age-old wisdoms of age-old bargains

V

Night has come and gone again
From the whispering echoes to the keen ear
The throes of a new tribe peals through the morning walls
Clear as might, bright as the shiniest model on display
Gone is the dependable clay base
Upon which nothing grows but craft
Onwards the march of tomorrow
Gathering light on a whale's hope
Peeling away the ironed skin on which dreams slide

VI

They left the song too late
But the half rhymes joined the march of days
Half blown by the rousing sweep of feet on rust
Tomorrow's people did not fade
In fact they turned and turned again
To a time to come, to a promise pouring from the lips
Of the bargaining throng

Line on line, hip to hip, the well-meaning people
Saw to the passing of the rite

VII
Today the yearning still beat on the heart
Today fading saffron flails in the wind, brightening the sun
On the station platform outstretched bodies hand over
Parcels of wrapped up wariness
On the station platform prayer beads change hands.

UNBOUND
(A GHAZAL)

(For my friends in Hong Kong)
Where? What remains of my life and love left broken?
How can the great plans of man leave so much broken?

My love carried off, to serve others' ambitions.
Hard hearted corvee, our matrimony broken.

The dreams man dreams range large. Vanity, even more.
Yet my dreams, with one edict, beaten down, broken.

They say to build up they have to dig deep, stakes in.
Building narrow-mindedness, words and backs broken.

They say to touch Heaven, man's fancies must reach up.
But Heaven sees only the stretched and the broken.

They say when done, it unites this fragmented land.
But walls never join, they divide, break the broken.

Devoted, fixed in purpose, they sing to the soil.
Prayers for blessings that it all stands unbroken.

Toil, a simple word, speaks miles and miles of sorrow.
Boulders on shoulders, backs crushed, knees and souls broken.

And blood, the one true cement to bind the unbound.
How else to hold together the ruined and broken?

Through it all, you my love my husband, remain gone.
No word, no news, no trace. My tears flow unbroken.

But how can I know? Heaven hides from me its tears.
For the fancies of great men must not be broken.

I see in my closed eyes, your sweat for man's vision
Of glory for one. But your bowl remains broken.

Kings and queens, warriors and heroes, are honoured, mourned.
Common folks' monuments are in soil barely broken.

Each man a brick, each man a load, each step fumbled.
These are better words. The history book's broken.

Their public words feed the chronicles, their lies cast.
Yet the truth of love and loss are never broken.

History, they say, is the fiction of empires.
Its human toll is redundant, records broken.

Greatness wanted the world altered, our lives improved.
Instead, themselves are changed. Ours unhinged and broken.

They who built had no will but finally believed.
We who've lost, we too must believe hope's not broken.

And hope alone must rely only on vague tales,
Rumours, hearsay, dark whispers, stories half broken.

Insinuations in half-light, like the dusk, leaves
Hope teetering between joy and joy broken.

My journey, my search, like the breach, are my last stand.
Among million men, million steps, a million broken.

We alone in our loss are alone together.
For this bricked snake, we millions of lives are broken.

It will stand, this pride and joy of generations,
Testament to ruler and ruled, rules unbroken.

They say to move Heaven, they have to dig deeply.
This grave keeps forgotten men who lay still, broken.

I say to move Heaven, we dig into our hearts.
Cry tears, drown sorrows, wet the blood of the broken.

Dear love, I cry into your bones. Sleep my loved one.
Our unity is two, your remains are broken.

Who weeps for the weepers, remember us who've lost?
History as good as the tale of the broken

Can be preserved by a recital of the ruined.
I will cry to Heaven to write from the broken

Tiles and bricks and mud and sand. My love could not rest.
Now his sleep is eternal, his dreams unbroken.

I, Meng Jiang, lay next to you, muddying history.
We who've lost, with tears and blood, can break what's broken.

SONG FROM THE CAVE

Now here is sense more suitable than
How, when they came for the roses
The half-heard promises
Stood singing in the ancient caves.

One morning rose the lined carriers
One new spirit one thrust
Exhorting
Singing

Of possibility that is infectious.
Of blind hope leaning, learning
Rolling, certain the chances are choices.

Success is a matter of taste,
They sing

So too the silence of quite a determination.

They still want their roses
Are still collecting
Promises of course
Now with fervour more suited to the
One note.

HAPPINESS

The tart dream

envelopes

the gateway

shrouded from

plain sighting

Stretched by the

manners of

felicitous

web weave borne

down by the

weight of its

own making

Not daring

a smile it

yet contends

Holding up

pillars, walls

HAND EYE BREATH

The designators of anatomy
Sits perfected harmony
Head, neck, chest, hand and six
Genuflecting to truth

The tonic of the heart
Beat mellow and mute
At length in intervals
And differences resolve

Resonant and reverberant
There being much
To be left unsung but
For the echoes

And love and faith.

HUMANITY'S FOOTSTEPS

Arise
Take the dyer's hand
It leads the way away
Dance the night dance
Scars do fade away
With the Nijinsky dream
Speak his fluidity
Grace of this humanity's footsteps
Arise, soar
The pieces go together
In this
Our dance.

PALIMPSESTS

Where goes the selfsame face looking
Out the canvas?
How count the promises of princely preambles?
In tears
Nothing needs hiding, the selfsame nameliness
Of one life imposed upon another
And a third and,
Consumed by the longing of the already now
Neptuned sea-shadow of cold doubt, how
To fight the light?
It is both more or less
It is either both or and
Not as if hopes only dwell in half-light
Not as if dreams belong only to the night.

ET TU …
A PRAYER
FOR CHING
O' LIM

BY JEREMY FERNANDO

Il lit sur mon lit
a phrase that came to me suddenly, in the middle
of nowhere
— as I was reading.

That
Perhaps even   I am always in bed when reading
For

                regardless of where I am; or even,
                whenever I read, a *he* that is me but
                not I (*moi, non je*) is in bed …

                          let's call him –*remy.*

Allowing all the possibilities of reduction to
resound in the background.
Where what is left after all of the wine has been
burnt is –*remy*
without ever quite being sure if what remains, the
remainder, is in the letters, or in the dash; *that*
which can only be seen but not heard, that hides
aurally from us but still leaves its mark, perhaps
always marks me.

Keeping in mind — or, at least, trying not to
forget — that dashes quite possibly dash us too,
break us apart.
Like rocks.
Though it might just be one's own fault: for, who
ever heard of drinking brandy on the rocks.
Where perhaps, dilution is precisely the call of
the sirens, where the sirens call through the very
melting itself.
Which is the danger that Odysseus was aware of:
for, it not the song that kills you — it merely lures
you with its beauty, its sadness. All one had to
do was to keep oneself from the water: that was
precisely the medium of death, what actually led
you to the rocks.

Or perhaps Kafka was correct:
« the Sirens have a still more fatal weapon than
their song, namely their silence. And though
admittedly such a thing has never happened,
still it is conceivable that someone might

possibly have escaped from their singing; but
from their silence certainly never. Against the
feeling of having triumphed over them by one's
own strength, and the consequent exaltation
that bears down everything before it, no earthly
powers could have remained intact ».

And that the frown on Odysseus' face — the
very sign that signaled to his companions they
could release him from the mast, the one that was
supposed to mark the fact that he was no longer
under the spell of the Siren's song — was due to
the fact that all he heard was their « silence ».

Which might well mean that even though
he escaped that time, the song is always also
awaiting him. Or, even worse, that each time he
sees water, the memory of the « silence », of the
possibility of the song, haunts him.

Even if he might have tried to put it behind him,
attempted to have forgotten.

For, as John Irving never lets us forget: « your
memory is a monster, you forget — it doesn't. It
simply files things away. It keeps things for you,
or hides things from you — and summons them
to your recall with a will of its own. You think
you have a memory; but it has you! »

Where each song, every song, any song — or, even worse, any silence, every silence — is quite possibly their song.

Awaiting the moment, their moment, to wash over him again.

Where perhaps, the very sound of death — if there is a sound to death — is the moment when the rocks and water collide: after all, should the Sirens have bothered with Odysseus, at least in their usual way, that might have very well been the last sound he would have heard.

Starboard stutterings stay still
World dissolving into knotted whispers
Of pretend goodbyes and good lord
Trading on the meeds of others
Unloading prosperity one at a time
One at a time

In the icy cold,
no less.

The swirling of ice in its melted self — always
proposing the possibility, the sound perhaps, of
death to –*remy*;
not quite smoke on the water,
but close enough.

Which opens the question — since the sound of
rocks clinking, clashing against each other, in a
glass is never far from me as I read, whenever I
am reading — leads us to the question, *what is
the sound of reading*, which always brings along
with it its compendium, its mixer, if you will,
what is the risk of reading.

For, if reading is an attempt to attend to the
possibilities of the text, the possibility that is the
text — to the text as other — it is always already
a response to another in which one cannot be
certain if one is picking up a call from the text,
or writing that very call into being. So, even if
one sees reading as a certain vocation — a *beruf*,
if you prefer — the very status of the *ruf*, the call
itself, is in question. Thus, the risk — at least one
of the possible risks — is that the very attempt
to read — for, if it is an approach, we cannot
conceive of it as an act, at least not necessarily so
— every try, any trying, perhaps even trial, is not
just haunted by misreadings, over-writings, one

cannot even underwrite it with the certainty that reading has taken place, that one has even read.

Perhaps here, it might be a good place to note that in English, it is impossible to discern whether the word *read* is in the present or the past: which might be no accident, considering the fact that one can never quite know if it has taken place, even if it might be happening at any given moment.

Which might also mean that the most appropriate form is the gerund: that one is *reading* prior to, during, after, opening oneself to the possibility of the text.

Thus — and here I am going to cite, recite from memory, risk an attempt at remembering a conversation with my dear teacher, Werner Hamacher from many moons ago, over lunch in Saas Fee, where he opened my registers to the notion that — « reading can no longer be constituted in the classical tradition of hermeneutics, as an act of deciphering meaning according to a determined set of rules, laws: this would be reading as an act where the reader comes into a convergence at best with the text. In fact, reading can no longer be understood as an act, since an act by necessity be governed by the rules of reading. Reading must be thought as the event of an encounter with an other —

an other who is not the other as identified by
the reader, but rather an other that remains
beyond the cognition of the self. Hence, reading
is a *pre-relational relationality*: an encounter
with the other without any claims to knowing
who or what this other is in the first place; an
unconditional relation, and a relation to no
fixed object of relation. As such, it is the ethical
moment *par excellence* ».

Bearing in mind — for, this is always a load
on one, should weigh on one, might even be
a burden that one can never rid oneself of,
especially if one is attempting to conceive, bring
forth, the possibility that reading and ethics
are potentially inseparable — bearing in mind,
trying never to forget, that in citing another, one
is always already pulling, ripping, wrenching,
the passage, the thought, out of context. Re-
contextualising — if one wants to be generous, be
kind to oneself, but really de-contextualising —
by putting it into one's text: so, not just a change
in context, but a theft, a kidnapping.

Where one steals (*voler*) by causing the text of
another to fly away (*voler*);
one might even say, *calling out to the text by way
of attempting to seduce the text, to lure the text to
one self.*

Vampirism:
taking the life of the text;
sucking the life from the inscriptions
making it one's own
for one's self

Which means that: in order to read ethically, to
have the possibility of an ethical reading, one
might well have to read without ever quite doing
so: *reading as an openness to the possibility of the
text*, in the precise sense of attending to the text
without ever quite knowing what this text is;
where the text itself — not just interpretations of
the text, for Hermes has long left the building,
but the *text qua text* — lies behind, is quite
possibly, a veil (*le voile*), remains veiled from one,
where it has perhaps long already sailed away
from one, where it is nothing other than a sail
(*une voile*).

And if, at this moment, one is feeling vain,
hubristic even, and wants to channel Socrates
— leaving aside the potential irony of doing
so — and claim that with enough thinking one
could sweep away such veils, and reach, or maybe
even glimpse, the *eidos*, one might keep in mind
the lesson from Led Zeppelin, the teaching that
escapes from the lips of Robert Plant when he
sings, « our shadows taller than our souls » :
where perhaps, all we can ever see are those tall
shadows, so tall they might not just stand over us,

but wrap around us, veil us. For, one should also try not to forget that the advice, solution even, to look out of the cave, into the light, might do us no better: after all, looking directly at, staring into, the sun only leads to blindness. Where one's eyes cloud over, become yet another veil.

It is perhaps no coincidence that the band that brings us this thought could only have been named after a sail that caught fire, that exploded, that burst into flames. After all a yardbird, even a new one, can only stay grounded: to leave the ground, one always runs the risk of flying too close to the sun.

And, at that moment, perhaps all one can say is:
« excuse me, while I kiss the sky ».

Thus, a reading that is not quite reading as if one is reading,
but *a reading that is not quite a reading*:
that is both reading and not reading at exactly the same time.

And if reading is to be conceived, at least momentarily, as taking a step towards the possibility of the text, a step towards the text as a possibility, this is nothing other than a step that is *un pas au-dela*.

§§§

I read without reading you;
for, it is impossible to read the words of you, a
dear friend.

Not because of the risk of erroneous readings,
of mistakes that might be made, of possibly
offending — nothing so banal; after all, a true
friend stabs you in the front. But because, whilst
reading you, I might accidentally resurrect you,
raise another you …

— surtout sur un lit —

Which leaves us with the question, the
unanswerable question: *which you have I
resurrected*. Or even, *which fragment of you has
been brought back*. Not that a fragment of you,
and *you*, are necessarily distinguishable: for, the
part that is read (whatever this may even mean)
and the parts that are unread are not so much
antonyms, but always already a part of each other.

Where reading is always already contaminated
by the possibility of *un-reading*. Or even more so,
that un-reading — which is not so much a not-
reading, but a reading that *un-reads* reading — is
not just the limit, but the very condition of the
possibility of reading itself: for, if there were ever
a total reading, a complete reading, completed

reading, there would then quite possibly be
reading no more.

Contagion is a branded, brand new, sorrow.
It beats and heaves and heaves again,
In surviving, survived none — refused all.
It heaves and beats again.

Or, perhaps even where reading, the attempt
to read — even if reading is the opening, the
openness, to possibilities, even if reading
attempts to maintain the otherness of the text
whilst engaging with it — the attempt to read
is precisely what contaminates the text itself.
For, even if the fragment and the whole are
indistinguishable — thus, the possibility of
multiple texts, a text as multiple possibilities
— each time one possibility is attended to, is
resurrected, all of the others are condemned to be
put aside, sentenced to death by the sentence that
one is drawing out, drawing from; the sentence
that is elicited through, brought forth by way of,
writing, even a reading out, sentencing all others
to a momentarily veiling. And since, we are
attending to the possibility of *reading as event*,
each sentencing is a branded, brand new, sorrow.

Where reading is always also entangled, entwined
with, loss, departure, mourning.

Which might be why — as Jacques Derrida
reminds us — *nous nous devons à la mort.*
We owe ourselves to death, one might say.
Where the *we* and *ourselves* are always already
separate in this debt that is owed to death.
Perhaps always separated by the very moment of
reflexivity itself, where not just that one is aware
of the self, but that in attempting to attend to the
question *who am I*, one is always also *reading*
one's self into being.

Thus, quite possibly always already mourning
one's self.

Nous nous devons à la mort.
Not even a question of choice, but an imperative.
After all, it is not as if one has any options when
it comes to debts.
Or, death.

So, even as I am attempting to write on,
attempting to attend to, the works, the thoughts,
of a dear friend — or even, giving in to the
temptation to write *for* a friend; for, one should
not attempt, there is no point trying to bother,
to hide the fact that this piece is a response to
a call from a dear friend, though a call that did
not originate from him — a question, a concern,
that is constantly resounding in the background
is: what is the *risk* of reading a friend; what is
the risk of responding to a call from a friend,

of running towards their call, running towards them when they call.

For, do we only dash to another if there is something in them, an element of them — even and perhaps especially if this element remains veiled — that we find dashing?

And in dashing towards them, towards another, do we also possibly dash them — at the very least, run the risk of dashing them?
Breaking them apart.
Precisely by coming too close.

For, if we pay attention to the beautiful reminder of Jean-Luc Nancy — that « it is space that one first needs in order to touch », to be in communication with — the erasure of this gap between does nothing other than to efface this communion. And in doing so, potentially effaces the other.

This is perhaps why it is crucial to maintain that the call to write, to respond, does not come from — does not originate, if you prefer to evoke the dossier of authorship, of authority, from — him, from Ching. That the author of the poems, of the text, is not the origin (*auctor*) of this call: and has not authorised — quite possibly never will authorise — this response, my reading of his, these, poems.

That it is all happening behind his back, as it were.

So perhaps, always with the hope — even if it might be a vain one — that the death that is owed, the *ourselves* that *we* owe to death might be that of the poem, or even poetry, but not the one who had first inscribed them.

Nous nous devons à la mort.

That the *ourselves*, the *we*, *nous*, that is owed to death might be what has come out of one, is brought forth by one — perhaps even by one's mind, intellect, *noûs*, νοῦς.

Not that poetry, the poem, and death, might quite be so separable.
For, after all, it not as if poems can exist beyond, outside of, the realms of reading and writing — the realms of mourning and death. And perhaps, it is at the very point of reading — and naught can be known of writing if it is not first read — that *ourselves* & *we*, *myself* & *I*, conjoin, become indistinguishable, again.

Nous nous devons à la mort
Ou, peut-être, nous nous devons à la poésie
Peut-être même à un poème
Comment on pourrait distinguer les trois — c'est
peut-être ça, le vrai mystère

So, perhaps what we might be attempting to think, the question that remains with us, is: what is this *space* between death, poetry, and a poem — which is also the question of *what is the space between reading and writing*.

That perhaps being *le vrai mystère*, the true mystery.

However, even when one knows about, learns of, the contents of a secret, what the secret contains, the secrecy of the secret — what is secret about the secret — perhaps remains secret from one; refusing to be secreted.

Car, le jour où les poèmes m'a coupé le souffle, je ne m'y attendais pas du tout.

For, one should try not to forget that to begin attending to something one must also cease one's attention from everything else: much like — to return momentarily to Werner Hamacher's teaching — listening entails ceasing to hear. In Werner's words: « why is the call thought of as something which, rather than taken, taken down, or taken in — be it from a specific agent, subject, principle, preferably a moral one — will be *given*? And if each call which issues is destined to make demands on the one who is called (but this is also questionable), is it already settled that I will hear, that I will hear this call and hear it as one destined for me? Is it not rather the case that the minimal condition to be able to hear something as something lies in my comprehending it neither as destined for me nor as somehow oriented toward someone else? Because I would not need to hear it in the first place if the source and destination of the call, of the call as call, were already certain and determined. Following the logic of calling up, of the call, of the *appel*, and along with that the logic of demand, of obligation, of law, no call can reach its addressee simply as itself, and each hearing is consummated in the realm of the possibility not so much of hearing as being able to listen up by ceasing to hear (*Aufhören*). Hearing ceases. It listens to a noise, a sound, a call; and so hearing always ceases hearing, because it could not let itself be determined other than as hearing, to hearing any further. Hearing ceases. Always. Listen … »

Which means that to attend, in attempting to attend to each poem, I have to listen to one — enact a *caesura* — whilst ceasing to hear any of the others, to cease hearing poetry itself, to withdraw from perhaps even attempting to tune in to Ching himself.

But even as one has to listen to the call of the poem — to tune one self to the call, to recognise that there is a calling that is taking place — it

is not as if one can ever quite be sure if one is
listening to a call or if there is a call only because
one is hearing it as such. Thus, even as « hearing
ceases », listening is quite possibly haunted
by hearing, by the whispers of hearing, by the
spectres of *here* in hearing: in that, only in the
space, place, that one has heard, that one thinks
that one hears, is there this moment that *one calls*
listening.

Where listening is not just a cutting off, a cut in
hearing, but that the naming of it as listening
is the very enactment of this cut itself — where
the cut is precisely in the moment that the very
thing that one is attempting to attend to catches
our attention: a moment — a *now*, if you prefer
— that is always already future-anterior; once
recognised, once listened to, always already in
memory, but always also in the *to-come*, as a
potential, in awaiting.

But, even if one knows this, even if one is fully
cognisant of this cut, *couper*, that has taken place,
one is never quite certain — even retrospectively
— of *when* it strikes one.

Or, if it even did;
for the cut could well also be self-mutilation,
a stabbing of the self.

Or perhaps it, it was always already there —

and all one has to do, all I had to do, was to
discover the mark of the cut,
its signature, the scar which it has left;
the cleft of the poem, as it were.

I no longer even remember — perhaps never ever
knew — which poem it was;
it could well have been all of them, or one of
them in place of them all.
All that I knew, was that my breath had taken
flight,
had been stolen from me.

But, in terms of being certain,
je ne suis sûr de rien.

Or perhaps, I do not want to see that I do not
want to see.
*Ou peut-être, je ne veux pas voir que je ne peux
pas voir.*
*Peut-être même, je ne peux pas voir que je ne veux
pas voir.*
Or, I cannot see that I cannot see.

Where, perhaps what I really can't see — as in
cannot bring myself to see — is the death of my
friend.

Even when I know that it will come, will always
come, perhaps has already come. For, it is not
as if we know what death is: and even whilst we

might all be waiting for death, it is not as if we know what or who we are awaiting; death might well have already claimed us, and all that we owe to her is the recognition, the realisation, that our self is dead, that we have always already been dead.

Even when I know that all I am doing is holding on to the promise that *Ms Death told me to tell you (s)he won't come this evening but surely tomorrow*.

And remain right here.

For, the fatal error — as the soldier who raced to Samarkand never gets to realise — is to try to flee death, to run away from her.

But, it is not as if one doesn't attempt anything at all.

After all, friendship itself is always already a risk. For, as Jacques Derrida never quite lets us forget, « to have a friend, to look at him, to follow him with your eyes, to admire him in friendship, is to know in a more intense way, already injured, always insistent, and more and more unforgettable, that one of the two of you will inevitably see the other die ».

Which might be why the phrase through which
I am attempting to think the relation between
a poem, poetry, and death — the phrase of our
debt to death — is a phrase that also comes from
elsewhere, from Derrida, as if — but one can
only hope that — *distance* works as a sort of an
apotropaic: if not elsewhere, at least here.

This is my wager — the risk that I take.

That by stealing his voice — not just Derrida's,
but also Ching's — by citing him, by invoking
his poems, as if he were the one writing them,
speaking them, saying them out, that by speaking
over him, by taking away his voice — through
prosopopoeia — Ching will not be able to answer
the call of death.

The fact that he is standing in front of me:
I hold on to the hope that Ms Death can *not* see.

§§§

Voices
Sounds. For, when do vibrations
become a voice.

Somewhat like the mystery of *finding one's voice*.
For, if it is to be found, it suggests that it is
potentially external to oneself — even if this
externality may have always been inside one. And
one sees this, hears this, in the colloquial phrase,
I found my voice: where the « I » that does the
finding is quite possibly not the same as the «
my » that is discovered. Where, once « found »,
whatever that might mean, there is no guarantee
that it has anything to do with the one that does
the finding; or perhaps, might well take over the
« I » that was there: where the *found voice*, as it
were, is precisely what does away with the « I »
who writes.

Which might well be the moment that Socrates is
speaking of: the very instant in which the *daemon*
whispers in one's ear, and where craft, *tekhnē*, is
transformed, moves, changes, shifts, form, into
art — where the craftsman possibly disappears.

Where the one who writes, where the « I »,
disappears.

L'instant de ma mort

> Where in *my death*,
> what disappears is nothing other than the « I ».

The lone walker hears the secrets of the wind and
the voices of the trees.
The path is not tongue-tied.
Here, strong lines persist, incanting, singing.
How does the judgement, what criteria persist
To keep the premise sound? It is written and shall
be read.

But, by whom?

That perhaps is not so much the question,
but quite certainly a question.

Keeping in mind Paul Celan's beautiful, haunting,
reminder that « *la poésie ne s'impose plus, elle
s'expose* ». One might even say it opens itself:
much like the *writing of light* which one can
only see after it lets itself be looked at. « But who
would be able to decide whether his is an art of
production or reproduction? », Jacques Derrida
asks of the work of Jean-François Bonhomme in
particular, and quite possibly of photography in
general: perhaps completely apt that exposure
can only be approached as a question; for, if what
is posed is outside of, is beyond, the object that is
opening itself to that position, anything that one

can see, that one can perceive, is quite possibly always also alterior to — both from and beyond — it.

And, if what is poetry lies in what is exterior, then what we are opening ourselves to when we attempt to see is quite possibly its remainder.

So, perhaps all that one can read — let alone write — is what remains of it, what remains with us, the remains of the rest, *reste le reste*, of what we call the poem.

For, as Michel Foucault teaches us, « in writing, the point is not to manifest or exalt the act of writing, nor is it to pin a subject within language; it is, rather, a question of creating a space into which the writing subject constantly disappears ».

Which is not to say that the subject can completely disappear.
Far from it.
Nothing quite so vain.

« As if the fullness of the soul », as Jooyong Choi might quip, « did not sometimes overflow in the utter vapidity of language ».

And perhaps, what remains of the one who reads is what is found in bed.

Is *me*.

As if, at any given moment, time, point — in
any given reading — the poem, Ching's poem,
whistles gently in one's ear, whispers — to echo
the words of Hélène Cixous — « I am for you
what you want me to be at the moment you look
at me in a way you've never seen me before: at
every instant ».

Even as it might be chuckling, perhaps always
laughing

le rire du poème

A laughter from elsewhere,
one that we perhaps cannot yet hear.
Much like the *silence of the sirens*. Always perhaps
already there,
awaiting us.

Where one might even posit: a laughter not
just from nowhere, thus everywhere — but,
more than that, perhaps also potentially from
everybody, everyone, thus also *nemo*, from
nobody. But not only in its Latin accent, but also
with another echo, a whisper from Gaul; that of a
sanctuary, of a certain *la demeure*.

Of a haunt, we might say, at least in English.

Keeping in mind that a haunt is both familiar, comforting, a place of repose, where one can be oneself, but — at the same time — what disturbs us, fills us with a certain dread, maybe even watches us, even as it might well be watching over us. Where familiarity — allowing all echoes of family to resound in the background — is the very moment where something comes too close, where the gap, space, for touching, for relationality itself, is ruptured, and where the effacement of the other, the consumption of the other by oneself, of oneself by the other, is what brings the unease.

Where perhaps what is haunting me is the fact that to write on Ching's poems — no matter how much one tries, how much I attempt, not to, no matter how much it may be the *me that is not-I* that is taken over by the poem, his poems, it is always also the I, or the « I », (the two remaining difficult, if not impossible, to distinguish), who signs off on the inscriptions, and hence one, thus I, should take responsibility for doing so — that to write on the work that is brought forth by or through Ching, is to always also write on Ching, over Ching.

Thus, an act of — in — fidelity.

Perhaps then, as I write, all that I am attempting to do is to write in prayer;

writing as a prayer, to request, to ask for;
ultimately, to ask (*fricgan*) —
not just writing a question,
but quite literally, writing as a question.

Where even as this is stated, even as I am stating
this, confessing this, one should bear in mind
Hélène Cixous' teaching that *one can only confess
to one that already knows*. For, confession is not a
matter of knowledge: one confesses as if the other
already knows of the transgression. Whether this
— both the confession and the transgression — is
true or not is beside the point: otherwise, it is
only a matter of revealing, of telling. Confession,
on the other hand, is a matter of asking for a
pardon, for forgiveness; regardless of whether
the other knows if (s)he has been wronged; a
matter of authorising the other to grant one this
forgiveness, even if (s)he never knew, even if
(s)he continues to remain in the dark after the
confession.

This is why confessions are always rituals, take
place through rites: for, it is not so much a matter
of what is being confessed, but the fact that a
confession takes place, that one has confessed.
In that regard, confessions are strictly speaking
meaningless: it is not their signification that
matters, but the significance that it has occurred.

Much like writing.

For, as Roland Barthes continually reminds us: « writing isn't beholden to truth and is, indeed, consciously accepted illusion — illusion, fiction, art — but, as such, it is, in the end, less mendacious than a discourse that lays claim, dogmatically, to truth ».

Thus, the notion of *written confession* is quite possibly tautological: for, the « consciously accepted illusion » is not just the space between that allows the confession to take place, to be potentially accepted, but also the very gap that opens the possibility that all writing confesses.

Not to anything in particular: for, even after a confession has taken place, what is confessed — the actual content of the confession — remains secret.

But, to the fact that the one who writes has — to the fact that *I have* — written.

So, perhaps all one can say of Ching is: he writes while he writes.
And all I can say of *me* is: *quod scripsi scripsi.*

And in my prayer for Ching O'Lim,
all I might be able to do is to ask questions, to
question, write in response — the two remaining
in a dance with each other — write to his name,
whilst attending to the echoes of the Hokkien
that resound with us as I write:

that to *Lim* is to drink.

And with all the risks entailed in being friends,
raise a gin & soda to him, to the work that comes
through and with him —
for, gin is the drink of our friendship.

CONTRIBUTORS

Britta Noresten is a visual artist, who paints and draws because she got fed up with her job at the bank. She graduated from The Florence Academy of Art, where she is now working as a principal instructor in drawing and painting. Her works have been exhibited at the European Museum of Modern Art in Barcelona, the Mall Galleries in London, as well as in her native Sweden.

Lim Lee Ching is a senior lecturer of literature at the Singapore University of Social Sciences. He holds a PhD from the National University of Singapore, and a BA from the University of London. His recent publications include a monograph entitled *The Works of Tomas Tranströmer: The Universality of Poetry*, and contributions to *Global Encounters: Cross-Cultural Representations of Taiwan* and *American Modernist Poetry and the Chinese Encounter*. He has published in several journals such as *Moving Worlds* and *The Journal of English and American Studies*. Lee Ching is also the founding editor of the *Singapore Review of Books*.

Jeremy Fernando is the Jean Baudrillard Fellow at the European Graduate School, where he is also a Reader in Contemporary Literature & Thought. He works in the intersections of literature, philosophy, and the media; and has written nineteen books — including *Reading Blindly*, *Living with Art*, *Writing Death*, and *in fidelity*. His work has been featured in magazines and journals such as *Qui Parle*, *Berfrois*, *CTheory*, *Full Bleed*, *TimeOut*, and *VICE*, amongst others; and he has been translated into Japanese, French, Italian, Spanish, and Serbian. Exploring other media has led him to film, music, and the visual arts; and his work has been exhibited in Seoul, Vienna, Hong Kong, and Singapore. He is the general editor of the thematic magazine *One Imperative*; and is a Fellow of Tembusu College at the National University of Singapore.

Mary Ann Lim is currently a student of Philosophy at the National University of Singapore who aspires to, in some near future, spend her days writing in her main preoccupations of film, poetry, and art, and sometimes altogether at once.

Neil Murphy teaches English and Irish literature at Nanyang Technological University, Singapore. He is the author of *Irish Fiction and Postmodern Doubt* (2004), and editor of *Aidan Higgins: The Fragility of Form* (2010). He co-edited (with Keith Hopper) *The Short Fiction of Flann O'Brien* (2013), and recently completed a four-book series related to the work of Dermot Healy, including a scholarly edition of *Fighting with Shadows* (2015), *Dermot Healy: The Collected Short Stories* (2015), *Dermot*

Healy: The Collected Plays (2016), and *Writing the Sky: Observations and Essays on Dermot Healy* (2016) — all with Dalkey Archive Press.

Yanyun Chen draws, and is driven by questions. These drawings have been exhibited in group shows in Singapore, notably at ChanHampe Galleries, Artistry, and Visual Arts Development Association. She is a Ph.D. candidate at the European Graduate School, where she completed her M.A. in Communications. She is a founding editor of Delere Press, teaches at Nanyang Technological University's School of Art, Design, and Media, and Yale-NUS College, Singapore.